The Things
We Give
Teeth

Poems by Geoff Young

Contents

Disclaimer

I'm only a poet at 4 am.

I'm only a poet when I have zero social contribution.

How High?

My legs get weak when I think about what love really is.

My shirt collars have been choking me for a while now.

My arms work as if they slip through different planes of existence.

They work, but not they way that they should.

I'm Trash

Maybe you wake up one day and you see just a little bit
too much grime leeching off of everything.

You slept in for far too long into the day and now it
seems as if it is gone.

The day isn't gone.

The day is a human construct.

The day starts exactly when the fuck you wake up.

It's not like anyone else can breathe fire regularly.

You can,

Some days.

Whatever you had to do today can wait the extra hour or
more you needed to sleep in.

That extra energy you had to cultivate.

Farewell, mi amore.

Farewell, syrup sweetness.

So get enough sleep, or don't.

Just don't let that be your excuse for not doing.

Please yourself in knowing exactly how much shit you
    can take before breaking.

Do a fucking thing, whether it's noon or midnight.

Do any fucking thing.

Drink that coffee.

Chase it, hours later with whiskey or vodka.

You're not here for them, you are here for yourself

And tough break, but shit,

Sometimes you won't like yourself

Or even feel like yourself.

Sometimes you owe it to yourself to not have it all
    together.

Sometimes, just sometimes.

It is alright to be a trash person.

Things I Learned The Hard Way

So I'm sitting there drunk out of my mind thinking about
   how you smile.

I'm wondering what you're thinking and the whole time
   I'm missing out on things I should be saying.

I'm missing out on you actually smiling.

I'm sitting there thinking about what we could be and
   forgetting about what we already have.

Hollow

Dressed up like a skeleton.

I've never been

that good with words.

We were all dressed up

like monsters

not caring what the neighbors thought.

We Are All Carnivores Pt 1

Such a carnivorous thing the heart is, it devours
     everything in its path.

If you were to set it free and point it's fury in the
     direction of what you want it would tear up rivers,
     bending and breaking everything and scorching the
     ground in its wake.

So why are we such timid creatures when we are
     powered by this indestructible and sustainable
     force?

Maybe we just can't truly fathom the uproar we could
     start.

Or maybe we are scared of that overwhelming shaking
     within our skulls.

Even after countless years writing about the will of the
     heart, most of us still don't live life with the engine
     of our emotions.

We bottle it, sell it, swim in it but we rarely live it.

We sink our teeth into it and pick the sinew from our
     canines.

It's not that we don't want to commit to it, it's just a
slow burn that we imagine we will have more time
to fuel.

So we kindle the things we don't need and extinguish
what's important.

How about you get out there and take those chains off,
let loose the monster that is the capacity of the
human existence.

Ala Carte

I

Don't

Know

When

It Was

That I

Stopped

Looking

Into

Peoples

Eyes

Awfully Gorgeous

The walls were crawling and the sun was shining. She was shining brighter and I couldn't see how I'd never noticed her here before. Everything around her felt dull. The wine in my mouth tasted bitter and lacking passion. She had drained the entire room. If I could have taken my eyes off her then I would've seen everyone else staring at her as well. The red dress she wore was like blood, her silver necklace like a knife. She was the culmination of all the thoughts and emotions of the evening. She embodied the entire nights jest. I was lost at sea, drifting through the masses of a party that had died, just trying to reach her. I felt cold away from her. I felt scared and alone. I brushed past beautiful girls and soaked in their envy for her. I brushed past princes and handsome millionaires who couldn't shake their fever and approach her. They couldn't get close to her, and I couldn't stay away. I stopped just shy of her grace and stared more intently. She didn't notice any of us, but we all noticed her. I stepped into the light she emitted. As if by cue she turned her head. Her long brown hair trickled down her neck and unto her chest. She saw me, and she walked away. How could I recover, how could I recall a time before this? She had been there for a blink of an eye, if every other person's gaze wasn't transfixed in the spot I was standing now I would believe that she was never here at all. Perhaps, they were laying eyes on me for the first time. I was out of place now, covered in an itch to flee; to follow her suit and disappear. I couldn't very well do that now that I was the object of interest. Had she passed some semblance onto my bones? Had she transferred her pretension onto me? How could I envision a future now that I had no past? The walls were crawling and the moon was shining. She was shining brighter and I couldn't see how I'd never noticed her here before. Everything around me felt dull. She mouthed words from across the ocean of blurred faces. "Run. Run while you still have the legs." One too many words were just enough.

I can't believe that side of me would ever show, especially so easily. I hid it so well; or so I had thought. With a crash and with a bang the world had ended, the music had stopped and the breathing had ceased. I'm not sure who you are but I had a grasp on the thing you had been. I was always open to the thought of being wrong. You flew so straight; like a god damned arrow. The precision you emitted was that of a goddess. When the news hit the shore you were the first of which people worried. Angles of an angel and wings of a demon, floating gracefully through the mist. Nothing touched you and if it could have; nothing would have held. I could have sworn that the clouds called your name. You were the ancestor of a different species; the fire of a different light. The thoughts came crashing in. My memory, your memories, came flooding in like a song. My eyes shattered, I swear to you that they broke. Tiny fragments of auburn and white piling on the floor by my feet. A piercing scream destroyed my thoughts. From the floor I saw them surround her. She broke the ranks and ran for the door. Each step she took caused her to descend into the marble. Her fingernails scratched the wood of the door as she faded downward and out of my mind. "Run. Run while you still have the legs." A voice screeched from below me. The clatter of glass on glass became too much for my wit to manage. I hurried for the door wondering why I had decided to leave. I leaned against the wall to gather composure. The walls were crawling and the chandelier was shining. She was shining brighter and I couldn't see how I'd never noticed her here before. I raised my voice to be heard over the music only to realize the music had stopped and the words wouldn't come forth. Her long brown hair trickled down her neck and unto her chest. She saw me, and she walked away.

Hard Not To See It

I passed out with an unlit cigarette in one hand and a half full Rolling Rock in the other. I dreamed about you, I dreamed about flying and I dreamed about zombies. Falling asleep is hard and waking up is even more of a tedious task. The room came back into existence and I held a half empty beer. See, the dream scape had changed me, I'd dreamed of you again and everything felt safe but this room, this barren room was cold and devoid of the passion that our sleeping thoughts give us. Things firing and colliding inside our heads while we slumber. This is why I write, this is why I breathe. Not for you and not for myself but for the passion of it all. For the monster sitting across the reading table staring with that damned smirk on its face. I write for each tooth in my mouth and I rinse with the water given to me by thousands of people before my time and even more that will follow. I wrote once for stability. Alas, that muse has moved along down the line and left my shaking palms too cradle this fire. A fire that sadly has a shelf life.

Nothing

There's nothing in the living room. There are couches and bookshelves and a nice coffee table your grandmother bought you 2 Christmases ago but really there is nothing in this room. Is this where you live? It's where you watch Netflix and sit in your own self pity but I'm pretty sure this isn't where you live. You've had people over a few times and you read a book every once in a little while but really is it a living room? I'm no expert on living, I do it in spans. Tiny sporadic moments of being in the here and now. So, that being said. Is it really your living room? What living have you done in there in the past week?

Month?

Year?

Do you have something else you should be doing other than sitting on the couch eating takeout and browsing the internet? I think we all could be doing more and I wish my mind were doing less.

The Color I Felt

I don't mind wasting time on you.

I will find a brighter hue

with you.

I know sometimes it's hard

but it's easy too.

I'm not afraid of anything in this tiny world. I'm not
afraid of anything but you.

I'll cough into the arms of my sweater

when I've got something to say.

I've been choking a lot nowadays.

You Are A Tempest

You are a tempest! You have to know that. You are a force, never to be taken lightly. I'm sure it feels sometimes, when you wake up in the morning deflated and insecure, that everything is so god damned difficult. What you have to realize is that; yes it is hard but sometimes it's easy too.

You're a collection of tremendous effort, experiences and forethought, so make sure that you aren't too hard on yourself. Don't let gravity hold you to things that will never fulfill you, she is a mistress so cruel and precise that you will be held to those convictions for a lifetime.

So, instead find things to hold you down gently, find things to caress your creativity and let yourself blossom into a living breathing human being. Drink coffee on the porch when it's cold outside to make yourself a more weathered soul. Drink beer in the front yard as the summer sun beats you down, to show you're still up for adventure, no matter how big or small. Take a shower, take a bath that lasts just a little too long and your fingers begin to prune. Break into a sprint for no good reason other than to feel the breeze. Can't let those demons catch you. The next time they rear their ugly snouts, you'll be too fucking fast.

You've trained for the bad days by enjoying the good ones to the fullest. Yeah, sometimes that might just make the shit days even more shit, but remember; You are a tempest!

Your Lips Are The End Of Me

Your touch is a bonfire.

Your fingers turn my bones to kindling.

Your tongue is a plague.

Your love is phantom.

I know exactly what it is.

Your lips are the end of me.

You splinter so wonderfully,

I'd swear you were glass.

Strike me over and over.

I've whispered your name for a thousand years.

Your tiny ears; they perk up at my words.

These gears that force my body to lift in the morning,

life's boring but you make it less a chore.

My run on sentences are going to be the death of me, but
I like to speak and you stare at these lips and your
lips are the end of me.

The end of the me who loved like greed.

The end of the me who stole hearts to flee and pleaded with itself after one too many fired up nights of debauchery.

The love I need, something heavenly, larger and heavier than I could lead. I bleed like nature made a forgery.

I sleep latched to the way you breathe and in moments of ecstasy you exist in me and your lips are the end of me.

I Don't Have Much To Say

I really don't have much to say.

I've tried being silent and that just seemed to rub me the
wrong way.

I've tried screaming about all of it but no one cares to
listen to anything.

No, a fusillade of unkempt words didn't seem to do the
trick either.

I've tried speaking slowly and into the microphone, the
static would crackle and cackle back at me.

I've tried regularly regurgitating other people's words but
no one finds quotes about the human experience to
have weight.

I've tried talking about myself like everyone else loves to
do but it turns out I'm not that interesting.

I've tried talking about current events but those just sting
and burn and lactate an uncomfortably familiar
ooze.

I've tried talking about how bad it's gotten but apparently
everything is fine and I'm just over analyzing
things.

I've tried singing it but even when I'm told I have a beautiful voice I can't shake the feeling.

I don't have much to say.

Put The Pint Down Kid

Alcohol isn't a romance it's a bastard with a knife. Jump too quick with that cigarette on your hand. It's a fun time with a loaded deck wouldn't want you to slip and break your neck, your bones aren't as strong has they once were.

I see the gears turning inside those eyes of yours. It's hard not to see in mine. The revered and the cultivated you got on your fourteenth year. The insides you used to wonder about just worry you now. It's a sick threat. This is who you are so drink up.

You can feel their eyes, It's not like you ever tried to thank yourself for getting here. It's just on everyone else's shoulders you made it to the top of the corpses. Of course it is, you don't have a strong bone in your body. The muscles in your mouth work on their own now.

Hookworm

I set myself on fire, drenched in the gasoline of our love.

I felt the flesh melt from bone and as I scooped and
      clawed at the scraps; I was rebuilt.

I wonder what this has felt like for others like us.

I am also selfish.

I hope we're the only ones to have figured out the right
      formula.

Noticing, your bones missing the important bits as well,
      we scraped together what we could from the
      floor.

We became whole again, respectfully, and in our own
      ways.

Then the question arose, where did you end and where
      would I begin?

We drank in the Thymol to kill the things inside us and
      feared to use the Epsom.

Sometimes it feels like I should rip my stomach from my
      body. There is something in there rotting me.

Something you've helped to calm.

I know the certainty of two things.

The first being that I will eventually cease to exist and the second that my love for you will not.

Curled into a ball

It's a rare thing for me to feel no pain. Pain is a
monarch. Pain rules over everything.

I don't mean the kinds of pain related to running yourself
out of air, for the fun of not being able to breathe
or bumping your elbow on that annoying corner at
work. I mean the kind that screams at volumes
over all the good in the world.

It's just...

It's just hard most days. Having your own pain crumpled
up into everyone else's pain. Hoping you can hide
your own long enough to help with all the others.
Hiding your pain long enough to realize yours is
not any more important.

Finding someone who puts their pain behind them and
you put yours behind you and you wait and hope
the pain doesn't come back a thousand fold. I'll just
quote someone more humble, brave and well put
together.

Be Here Now.

I Never Had This Problem Before

I never had this problem when I was single. I never had
to worry about staying up too late and waking you
up.

I never had to defend myself.

I never had to think about my health. I never had to
decide what I was going to do during my days and
nights weeks in advance. I never had to think about
where my money was going or how much I was
drinking myself to death.

That's exactly why I love you.

I care about you enough to get the proper amount of
sleep. It is good to defend oneself but I need
someone to call me on my bullshit. I have to take
better care of myself because my life is about more
than just me now. My life has become a little bit
more structured and you give me fun little
adventures to go on.

I have to think about our future, a future I want so
immensely. I can't drink myself to death because
I'll be missing out on time with you. I never had
this problem when I was single but fuck I had a lot

more pressing issues that you've helped me work
through so

Thank you so much. Thank you for being perfect.

Thank you for being you.

Straight To The Chopping Block

The night air felt so rigid and the grass scratched our skin like a thousand tiny knives.

I'd like to dress up so fancy, to the nines and what not, and just lay in a field with you.

We could slowly become the grass, slowly lose ourselves to the smallness of it all.

I'm not a statue any more. I move like fluid in and out of consciousness, I breathe like someone larger than myself.

Off in the distance somewhere you could hear a dog howl at the moon if you stopped and let your little heart go. I'd trace your collarbone down to your belly button; trying not to make you flinch. Gentle like the breeze that would help me do my work.

The wine we brought fails to keep us quiet.

We scream our insecurities into each other's eyes.

I wake in the morning to squeeze you. I'd never break you no matter how hard I've tried. It's a visceral thing, our love. I've lost my head. I swear it's like a guillotine.

Paralogize

You know that pesky, dripping, black sludge that loves to keep you down? The one that oozes through every orifice and into your thoughts. You may know this sludge well or you may just barely be able to imagine it. Either way, I'm telling you that you can fight back. Maybe even win. As I'm writing this, I'm writing with this thing on my shoulder. I've never been happier to be alive yet that toxic blob still sits there laughing at my happiness but that's ok, I let it howl and giggle because I've gained the tools, over the years, to combat this silly depression. Yeah, call it names because it can't hurt you more than it already does. Describe your depression, take away just a tiny bit of its power. For me it's just this glob of dark mass that trickles everywhere I go. It's got too many teeth and no eyes because it doesn't care to see what it does to me or the people around me. It only wants to feed and it is well fed. I let it in just enough because in a small way I'm in love with my own sadness. I'm in love with the way it makes music for me and the way it writes; all vigor and passion. I'll tell you, as someone you should probably never listen to, to use this illness in the same way it uses you. Whether it's anxiety, depression, OCD or any other frightening creature, you've got to fight back just enough to call it a draw. You can't ever truly win because that's when it comes barreling back into you like an atom bomb. I know this all sounds a bit futile since I'm telling you that you can't win. What I'm saying is you can't find yourself in a false sense of victory with these things. This is your life, go out there and tame that madness!

Untitled 1 (Writing; Hung Over In The Back of Mellow Mushroom)

We started a holocaust of feelings.

We formulated it spark by spark and by the end we sat amongst a blaze of emotion.

Some too dark to comprehend;

Others as bright as the god damned sun.

So we stayed, letting the flames lick our skin, letting the fire caress us all the way through.

If there is a soul in each of us then ours were burnt to ashes in a flicker of desire.

It's not something we'd necessarily regret or change. It was too late to turn back now, we were empty, we had poured it all into this ritual and the ritual had been very thirsty.

We Are All Carnivores Pt 2

Jagged, all shining and white, your incisors caressing my cheeks.

Letting out a whimper like a wounded animal I prepare for the bite.

Your pristine jaws take away a good portion of my flesh.

I breathe deep to help contain my exuberance for you.

Slowly tracing down my clavicle you take another hefty piece of me for your collection.

Your piercing eyes have set on my navel.

I am lackadaisical as blood from my wounds pool as you drink me in.

Taking your time quenching your thirst before walking your tongue to my feet.

You have feasted on all of me.

I am no longer whole.

The Things We Give Teeth

Isn't it strange the things we give teeth?

Our words all bloated and red.

Eagerness to leave crowded areas,

an itch straight through to the brain.

The books we read and the whiskey we use to scar
　　　ourselves.

The people we build to be monsters or gods.

Our tiny fingers gently scraping the sky

and

not so gently pulling down the stars.

Poor bastards.

The teeth on our tongue,

drawing blood from which we write myths and mayhem.

All the things we give weapons.

What power is in our eyes that we recklessly throw
　　　about?

Starving for flesh, we bite each other's lips.

Drawing blood from which we write myths and mayhem

The tiny lies we tell ourselves and others.

Invisible scratches on the inside of our brains.

Blasphemy clasped in your fragile hands.

How could we not have contempt?

A deity who wades through glass shards and is never cut.

For I never want to be hurt?

I want to live forever.

I want to see the last little flicker.

I want to stand on the edge of nothing and see
        everything.

Isn't it strange the things we give teeth?

Isn't it strange the things we give wings?

We are the only creature that creates monsters.

We created god once during a weekend trip to Boone.

I created another one the following week when I poured
        my soul out onto the shoulder of something that
        didn't love me.

I murdered a whole town of heroes.

I wonder if ghosts cease to exist when we leave the
room.

Does our love float about in the same fashion?

Or does that too linger within the creaks and groans of an
old house.

Do you miss me or have you already given me teeth?

The Color You Felt

I'm awfully full of fondness for others when I'm happy.

When I'm sad, I wish to expand the widths.

I'm just sad,

sad and tired

but I'm alive.

I'm Sorry

I'm such a fucking fool.

A jester.

King and Queen's Court and all.

So there's that.

You still managed to fall in love with me,

and I with you.

A small part of me sometimes feels like that was the most foolish thing I could've done.

But then the giant engine that drives me puts that to ease.

It was most definitely the least foolish kiss I've ever had.

I trace it back to the smell of cigarettes and a hum of electronic music.

You looked so beautiful, cradling that bottle of wine like it was your anchor.

I was a fool for every moment I hadn't dropped to my knees and prayed to you.

I was a fool for every moment I apparently let slip away from me.

I'm a fool now for writing this, a fool for speaking it into existence.

I wonder how foolish I'll feel in a couple years, reading this in the book I'll never publish.

So I guess missing you is a under statement and bookshelves are meant to be filled.

I'm

still

the

sleepy

person.

Coming Out

He was sitting there soaking his crackers in Jack
Daniel's

        while murmuring about how dead his brain
felt.

                All I wanted to do
was kiss him.

Secret Romance

Death, you fickle sack of shit.

Death, you beautiful goddess.

I'm not sure who you are today.

You're under my teeth.

You're in my veins.

That black sludge that I've convinced myself I would bleed.

The ingredients for life.

The same things go into death.

Death, you luxurious commodity.

Death, you vulgar misuse of power.

I just wanted to speak with you today.

You won't pick up your phone, I only needed you to listen.

Did you give me a wrong number?

Will I live forever, or would you like to come around after work for cocktails?

Tell me I'm as beautiful as you are.

Sometimes I just need to be held.

Death, how dare you pretend we never had that conversation.

Death, you liar.

I'm sorry for taking up your time.

I feel strangely lost without the fear of you.

I've become consumed with other things.

I just wanna say thank you, for everything you've done.

I've got your address.

I'll send you a postcard or something.

601

I threw out my mattress, a grand gesture.

I would've rather set it on fire.

I threw out tiny pieces of myself I'd collected over the
years.

More things that I thought I'd never need again.

I bought books to fill shelf space I've never had, an
emptiness I thought I'd never see again.

I held my best friends baby in my arms, I thought you
said " I looked so cute" but maybe I'm not
remembering that correctly.

I gave up meat, not really for myself, more for our
future.

I did a lot of things for you.

Ginger Ale and Oreos.

I did a lot more things for myself because of you.

This won't be one of those love lost poems because you
know, we'll still be friends.

I'll slowly relearn how to be an idiot and you'll slowly
learn how to climb mountains.

What I'm saying is you'll find something else on some
summit somewhere and I'll be starving.

Fuck mountains.

You'll learn to love yourself and there won't be enough
space in there for me because you've got so much
too love that you just haven't seen yet.

If you were writing this poem it would be about things
yet to come. Things on the horizon.

I guess for me this is a poem about love lost in the desert.
So far away from home that I can't seem to find it.
A love lost somewhere out there on it's own.

Chances Are

I remember this one time in high school, while reading "Things Fall Apart".

I was assigned a smaller copy of the book so the page number broadcast by the teacher never aligned itself with where I was in the story.

I feel lost a lot and I wonder if that's where it all started.

Untitled 2

I'm a gargantuan waste of space because I love too much,
    I love until I splinter.

Within those frayed ends I love even deeper.

In it's nihility I starve.

I love like a matchstick.

Powerful and blue but only for a moment and then I love
    like the cigarette my love lights.

Slow burn.

I'm never given the chance to love for an eternity.

The amount of intensity I have could flood the fucking
    earth, but I'm limited to these tiny bursts.

Limited by you.

Red Maple

My sweet forever.

Creating artwork on my arm with leaves.

She's vegan.

She still managed to take their lives.

More importantly she took mine.

I felt distant as if I were in a coffin.

I jokingly said we should have sex in the grass.

I didn't know until later that night why she was acting
    abnormal.

She says seeing my things hurts but I'm not sure why.

Is it because she longs for me or is it because she longs for
    my ghost to be gone from her house.

A house we were going to share.

So she can act like I never happened?

Her answer was deafening.

She cared but that wasn't enough

For all the lies you told me.

Under the guise of love.

Coals burning hot but never searing.

Killing me would've been more kind.

I'm Still Foolish In Love

He stared, foolish on Love.

　　She said "I'm going to get dressed."

　　She seemed to glide away, effortlessly becoming the past.

Only once did he think " It's okay; she loves me."

Never did he think "It's okay; we will remain friends."

There were too many pauses within her responses. She
　　felt weight, weight that held her sternly in place.

He hoped she just couldn't explain it.

He thought she just wasn't in love.

　　She moved her bed into the middle of the room
they had briefly shared. It was the way they first placed
the bed; the way he had wanted it to stay.

But she liked to sleep against the wall?

But she was scared she'd fall off in her sleep?

Oh God! She didn't have him there taking up space any
longer, so she could sleep in the middle of her bed

Which had become their bed; now was stripped of that
title. He was stripped of his title.

Epilogue

And

It

Snapped

                                                  Within

                                                  My

                                                  Hands

My

Trust

For

Anything

Thank you,

        to anyone and everyone who decided to read
"*The Things We Give Teeth.*" *It* means the world to
me because I believe myself to be probably the
worst poet or writer ever. That being said, I've
been told to put my work out there by many
people that I have loved or trusted. This is for all of
you. This is also for myself.

That's what this is.

www.ingramcontent.com/pod-product-compliance
Lightning Source LLC
Chambersburg PA
CBHW021146020426
42331CB00005B/929